NEXT-LEVEL

DIGITAL

NOMAD

A guide to traveling and working from anywhere
(even with kids and a day job)

Maria Surma Manka

Workation Woman

TABLE OF CONTENTS

"It's too bad you have to work when you travel!"

I've heard that comment more than once. And yet it's always surprising that someone pities me for spending weeks working and living in another country, immersing myself and my family in the daily life of another culture!

The point of a workation – "work" + "vacation" – is to do exactly that: To combine a love of travel with the reality and stability of work. Workations allow our family to travel for longer periods of time than we could normally afford to if we were just taking a vacation. We get the best of both worlds: The chance to see the world while still earning our regular income.

Workations take the idea of being a digital nomad to the next level. The stereotype of a digital nomad is someone who is young, unmarried, no kids, no mortgage, etc. A workation is a reimagining of what it means to be a digital nomad. It's a totally different type of travel experience that has its own benefits: You get to really know a city because you're commuting to work, going on lunch breaks with office mates, making deeper connections, watching or reading the local news and getting a stronger sense of the ebb and flow of life because you're more embedded in the city's fabric than when you're a tourist.

Think about it: As a tourist, you feel the pressure to see and do everything in such a short period of time. You go from museum to historic site to the restaurant your best friend said you MUST eat at to the beach to some hike that's ranked on some list on some website. On a workation, you get to slow down, take in your surroundings, and embrace the spontaneous. Some of my best workation memories are little places or events that were never part of a plan and that never appeared on any "must do" list.

Plus, a workation forces you to change your entire routine for a period of time. When else do you get an opportunity like that? You change your home, your food, where you grocery shop, where your kids play, where you work. Every major aspect changes – and that is thrilling.

A typical day on our London workation: Husband and I get ready for work while kids prepare for a city adventure with the nanny.

My Story

I live in rural Minnesota with my husband and two young boys. In 2013 I read Tim Ferriss' <u>Four-Hour Work Week</u> (4HWW) and was so excited by the possibilities it presented. The book is premised on the idea that time is the most valuable resource we have – not money. Its tactical, how-to approach walks through specific ideas for creating online businesses or other ventures that allow you to take "mini-retirements," which basically means you go away for several months to pursue projects or adventures you've always wanted to do, and work a minimum number of hours doing it.

Although the book's idea of mini-retirements was not financially or logistically realistic for me, I did see the possibilities of being location-independent - of being able to do my job from anywhere in the world. I thought perhaps my husband's work could be location-independent, too.

> But I had two very young kids at the time, ages 1 and 3. But I had a spouse with a regular job. But I'd just started by own public relations consulting business. But I had car and house payments. I didn't feel like I was in any position to travel for the foreseeable future.
> BUT BUT BUT.
> But...after reading the 4HWW, doing some research and brainstorming, I couldn't stop thinking about the idea of working while on vacation. I looked for resources to help me plan a workation, and I didn't find much. There are lots of website and books that tell you how to quit your job, sell your house, homeschool your kids and travel the world. There are also lots of sites to help you plan your dream vacation.
> What if you're somewhere in between? What if you just want to shake up your life for a few weeks or months out of the year, and not drastically uproot your whole family?

Becoming a Workation Woman

About 15 months after the idea was sparked, after about 80 hours of planning, after dozens of sleepless nights and many enthusiastic conversations with my husband, we left for four weeks to live and work in Barcelona (our boys were 2 and 4 by that time). A year later, we spent six weeks in Wellington, New Zealand. Two years later, we headed to London. I was self-employed the entire time, but my husband had two different employers from which he asked permission to work remotely.

Even after three workations and so much planning, I still haven't found good resources to help guide a typical family who wants to combine travel with their day job. And I've lost count of the number of people who have said to me, "I'd love to workation like you, but I don't even know how to start planning."

That's why I started Workation Woman (www.workationwoman.com), a website that gives ideas and resources to families who want to take on the workation adventure but aren't sure where or how to start. And that's why I wrote this book: To help people – especially families – figure out how to spend several weeks or months living elsewhere without quitting your regular jobs or significantly disrupting your lives.

I've surveyed Workation Woman fans and talked to dozens of families to better understand how to make a workation possible for a variety of family situations. This book is not filled with fluff or motivational quotes. It's a practical and tactical how-to guide that will help you kick-start your workation planning:

- Guidance for thinking through the trickiest questions when it comes to living and working abroad temporarily, like how to ask your employer to work remotely, preparing for the kids' absence from school, where to find a place to work and how to find child care
- Get a bunch of step-by-step worksheets to help guide you and make your planning efficient
- Save you dozens of hours of planning and dozens of sleepless nights worrying!

Why our family loves workations...

Maria
"My favorite memories are the ones we didn't plan or that don't show up on my list. Like the neighborhood yoga studio we joined, exploring the grocery stores (trying all the sweets!), or the gun salute in Hyde Park for the Queen's birthday."

Joram

"The experience of feeling like you actually live there. On our most recent workation, I rode a double-decker bus to work with all the other bleary-eyed commuters; and yet I could go visit Abbey Road Studios or the Tower of London on my lunch break. A workation is a feeling of normalcy and novelty at the same time."

Son #1 (age 8)

"The long plane rides because we get lots of food and can play games the whole time!"

Son #2 (age 6)

"I like having an upstairs in our new house!"

" A workation is a feeling of NORMALCY AND NOVELTY at the same time. "

Using this Guide

I'll take you step-by-step through the planning and execution of a workation – whether you choose to go abroad like me or you want to head to Florida or the Rockies for a few weeks.

You can read this guide from start-to-finish or you can skip to the chapters where you need the most help planning. This guide is especially pertinent to international travel with a family because that's been my experience, but many of these tips can easily translate into domestic or solo travel. If you work through this guide from start to finish, you will know:

1. How to ask your employer for permission to work remotely
2. How to work with your children's school leading up to and during the workation
3. Where to workation
4. When to workation
5. How to find a work space while workationing
6. How to budget and plan out costs
7. How to find a caregiver for your children or how to help them keep up with school work
8. When you should begin planning each step
9. How and what to pack

Keep in mind: This is a guide, not a manual that you have to follow. You have to make your workation fit what your family needs and wants. Maybe that's heading into the woods of the Pacific Northwest for a few weeks or maybe it's spending six months in Paris.

You get to choose your own adventure.

CHAPTER 1

Am I Ready for This?

"I want to do what you do,
but I don't know where to start."

Whatever a workation looks like for you, I guarantee the changes will result in permanent shifts in how you think about your life, routine and priorities when you return home. You ARE ready for this and this book will help you start planning your new reality!

A workation does not have to be a multi-month move overseas. Maybe you want to live on a lake for the summer and work from there. Maybe you want to avoid the winters in your home state and be a snowbird in Florida. Or, maybe you want to spend two months in Prague. Whatever a workation looks like for your family, it's time to get started!

Get outside of your comfort zone and open yourself – and your family – to moments you'll never forget and experiences that could change your lives forever.

> ### *My Story*
> *One of the things I love most about workationing is watching how people around the world parent their children – and learning from those differences! One day we were at this beautiful sunny playground*

next to the blue waters of Wellington Harbor in New Zealand. New Zealand playgrounds in general were higher and more complex than anything we'd seen in the United States and this structure was in the shape of a giant ship. I saw a young child (about two years old) up on the tallest part of it. I immediately looked around frantically for the parent, thinking "Do they know their kid is six feet in the air, hanging off the top of this ship and they could fall at any second?" I was literally about to start running around the park yelling, "Someone's kid is too high up!"

But I breathed easier when I saw the father walk up to the boy and grab him around the waist – and push him higher up the ship.

I'll never forget that moment. How many times do we pull our kids down and tell them "be safe" when we should be pushing them up and saying "go higher, I'm here to catch you?"

And for that matter, how often do we tell ourselves "be safe" when we should be saying "it's time to go higher?"

Visiting the Hobbiton movie set, New Zealand.

CHAPTER 2

Asking Permission from Work

"How do I ask my boss if I can work
remotely?"

The first step to take is figuring out if working in another location is possible. Of course, there are jobs that you simply can't do remotely for a few weeks. I get it. But if you're reading this book, you probably think there's potential to get out of the office for a while.

Many employers are open to employees working remotely. It's becoming a standard benefit at employers of all sizes and industries. Consider these stats:

- A 2015 Gallup poll found that 37% of American workers have worked virtually in their careers, a 30% increase in the past 10 years.
- The latest GlobalWorkplaceAnalytics.com research found that 40% more U.S. employers offer flexible work options than they did five years ago.
- Employers save on costs when employees work from home. According to the latest State of Telecommuting in the U.S. Employee Workforce, allowing a worker to work remotely half the time can save an employer more than $11,000.

If working remotely is the norm or has potential at your place of employment, start the conversation with your supervisor or boss at least a year out. And come prepared with a plan: Know how you're going to handle upcoming projects, team meetings or ent work, and be available at your regularly scheduled work times. You could suggest you do a test run for a week or two to prove that it will be seamless for your employer, coworkers and clients. For instance...

> *"My family and I have the opportunity to live in [location] next year for [amount of time]. I'd like to do a test run of this idea this summer and work from home for a two-week time period. I've got a plan that addresses all of my responsibilities and projects so I won't miss a beat."*

Get creative when thinking about the parts of your job that you could do remotely.

- Are you in sales? Could you schedule all of your in-person meetings in the first week of a month, and then do all of the paperwork or follow-up communication from California or Capri for the last three weeks?
- Are you someone who works with people face-to-face, like a therapist or coach? Could you plan for video conferencing for a few weeks while you work from Maui?
- Does your industry have a slow time? Could you spend that time living and working from a mountain retreat or lake cabin?
- Could you schedule time for that Big Project you never seem to have time for, and work on it from Tokyo?
- Does your employer have other offices you could work out of? Even if it's just one state over from yours, the opportunity to prove yourself trustworthy enough to work remotely could lead to more distant travel destinations next time.

There are a lot of great resources out there for planning to ask an employer about working remotely. Check out these articles from people who know what they're talking about:

How to Convince Your Boss to Let You Work from Home (Harvard Business Review)
How to Convince Your Boss to Let You Work From Home (same article title as the one above, but this one's from Glassdoor)
Exactly what to do to Convince your Boss to let you Work from Home on Friday (Fast Company)
Want to Work from Home? Here's How to Ask Your Boss (The Muse)

Working from a café in Catalonia, Spain.

My Husband's Story: Getting Permission from his Employer

When I first broached the idea of a workation to my husband Joram, he didn't bat an eye. I think his actual response was a nonchalant, "Sure, that sounds great! Let's do it!"

At the time, he worked as a marketing director for a small manufacturing company that was more than an hour drive from our house. Because of the commute, he was working remotely three days a week. About seven months before our departure, he broached the idea to his boss about working internationally for four weeks. To his boss' credit, where Joram worked didn't make much of a difference. As long as he got the work done and nothing fell through the cracks – including a major new website relaunch.

Our plan was to be gone for four weeks to Barcelona, and one of those weeks would be a true vacation to Austria. So Joram would work remotely for a total of 21 days. Since he was already working three days a week remotely, it was only an addition of six extra remote days.

He made sure his projects that required person-to-person time were handled before he left, and all conference calls or status calls would be held at the same time. The website relaunch – managed from overseas – was a success.

Two workations later, Joram had a different employer and his job required him to be much more in the weeds with day-to-day work, plus he had conference calls for up to four hours a day. When interviewing for the job, he told each interviewer about our family's workation tradition and that he planned to keep working overseas temporarily. None of the interviewers balked at the idea, and Joram was hired.

About a year later, we went to London for six weeks. We chose that location specifically because his employer had an office there from which he could work and get easy access to work files and resources. He met new coworkers and had opportunities to socialize and get the locals' take on what to do, see and eat. Best of all, it was a completely seamless experience for him and for his U.S.-based colleagues; including when he completed the largest project of his career from there.

Have specific questions? Need to brainstorm? Drop a note on the <u>Workation Woman Facebook page</u>!

CHAPTER 3

Getting Permission from School &
Keeping up with School Work

"There's no way a school will let you
pull your kids out!"

We started taking workations when our kids were in preschool, so pulling them out for 4-6 weeks wasn't a big deal. We hoped to continue taking workations even when the boys were in school, though several people warned us that a school would never excuse a child for so long!

But we asked anyway.

During our London workation, our youngest son was in preschool and our oldest was in first grade. It was no problem to pull out our preschooler, and I even asked for and received a prorated tuition amount for the time we were gone. That was some nice "extra" money to use toward workation expenses.

For our first grader, I was a bit unsure of how it would go, since we hadn't pulled kids out of the public school system before. And I didn't have any interest in homeschooling while we were abroad.

Our workation was planned for April through May, so the summer before (right before we booked our plane tickets), I emailed the principal, explained the opportunity we had to travel and work in London, and told him our first grader would have a nanny who would ensure he did his core school work (reading, math) every day. "Are there any red flags or negative consequences if he is gone for six weeks?" I asked.

The principal replied that very same day: "That should be fine. Have fun!"

My son's teacher was equally enthusiastic about the workation opportunity and even did a class lesson on London before he left (my son learned a lot from that!). I am so grateful for the teacher's and principal's support and their understanding that education is more than just the classroom experience.

Your school may be less forward-thinking about letting a child go for so long. In that case, be sure you have more of a plan.

1. Lay the groundwork: Establish a relationship with your children's school before you talk to a teacher or principal about pulling them out for a long period of time. If no one knows who you are, will they trust you to make sure your child stays on top of their lessons? Spend some time at the school when you can, even if it's just attending conferences. Putting a face and a personality to your request will help your cause.
2. Know the testing times and semester or quarter schedules: If mandatory testing happens in April, then schedule your trip around that. Or perhaps the school will recommend you travel within the same semester or quarter rather when the semesters or quarters overlap. Knowing these things ahead of time will make it less stressful for you, your child and the teacher.
3. Present ideas to the teacher on how the arrangement could work and make it as little of a burden on them as possible – they have enough to do! Will you have a nanny or a tutor who can help your kids stay on top of their subjects (many nanny agencies also offer tutors)? Are your kids old enough to do most of the school work on their own, with the occasional guidance from you and check-ins via email or Skype with the teacher?

If you're taking a workation in the same country in which you live, see if you can enroll your kids in the local public school. I know a family who spends half of the school year in their home state and the second half of the school year in California, and their daughter simply switches between schools. Other ideas:
- Is your current school affiliated with a larger network of schools, such as a religion or a teaching method like Montessori, and are there schools in your destination city your kids could attend temporarily?

- Search the web or Facebook for parents' groups in the city where you will live. Follow the conversations or ask for recommendations on daycares, nannies or schooling ideas.

Keeping up with school work.

Don't forget to keep clear, age-appropriate communication with your child during this time as well. They may not want to miss school or their extra-curricular activities, and they need to understand why this travel opportunity will be life-changing (even better, have them help plan workation activities related to their passions, like taking in a soccer game, visiting a theater or taking an art class).

Make sure the kids understand that a workation is not an extended vacation: Like you, they are expected to work during the week and keep up on their classes. The upside is that they will be surrounded by life-changing opportunities and have more control over their school day schedule!

For a real-life example of workationing with school-aged kids, check out my interview with Nichole about her family's two-month workation in Maui. She began talking with the school a year in advance (her children were in middle school and high school at the time). She used a combination of online classes, homeschooling, and class substitutions (studying marine biology for science class) to make sure her kids didn't fall behind. When the family returned to the States, their transition back to school was seamless – except for her daughter, who was actually a week ahead of her classes!

Other resources
Is It Okay to Pull Your Kids Out of School for a Family Vacation? (it's about vacations, but lots of the info is relevant to a workation)
Educational Travel: How to get Permission and Justify the Experience to your Local School

CHAPTER 4

Where and When

"How do you decide where you go and when?"

The world's a big place and it's exciting to have the entire planet to choose from! But when you're traveling with kids and working at the same time, there are some big factors that can help you narrow down a destination. After taking several workations with my family, here are some tried-and-true factors that work well for us.

Set an intention: Know WHY you want to workation
A workation requires a lot of planning, financial discipline and an honest examination of what you value. Thinking through why you want to workation and how you want to live will help you quickly filter through the unending choices of where to go and what to do. What is your intention for the trip?
- Is it important to expose your kids to a new language and culture?
- Is outdoor adventure important?
- Do you want to explore where your ancestors came from?

Take a moment now to write down your WHY on a card. You may want to put in on your fridge or another place as a reminder of what you're working toward. Or tuck it away in another safe spot that you can refer back to. When you start feeling overwhelmed by the planning or when you get really nervous the day before you leave (because you will), come back to your intention.

My Family's Intention

We live in a very rural area on +85 acres. Our driveway is almost a mile long and our nearest neighbor is a half-mile away. Our workation intention is always the same: to flip our lifestyle. We want to live in a large, bustling city that's noisy, smelly, crowded, and rich in culture, diverse in people and deep in history. We want to show our kids that different isn't scary; that it's fun and interesting to be surrounded by people who don't dress like you, look like you or speak like you. And that making mistakes – like ordering the wrong food or getting lost – is ok. And that the unknown – like exploring a city without having a plan or knowing what to expect – is fun!

If you have young kids, be prepared for people to say things like, "Your kids aren't going to remember this, so why are you doing it?" If I followed that logic, I wouldn't do ANYTHING unless my kids remembered it, including reading to or playing with them! Also, remember that parents don't have to make every life decision based on their children (shocking, I know).

My husband and I workationed because we had the means and ability to travel, and we took the opportunity to do it for US.

> **We want to show our kids that DIFFERENT ISN'T SCARY**

From rural Minnesota to downtown Wellington: Enjoying a very different view!

<u>Factors for choosing where to go and when</u>
Start thinking through these questions to figure out where you might want to go and the time of year you want be gone.

*At the end of this book, in the Appendix, use Worksheet A: Choosing Where and When to work through these questions and get pro tips from my own experiences. These worksheets are also available as printable, PDF files at **www.workationwoman.com**.*

<u>Do you have personal connections in a cool location?</u>
Explore where your personal connections could take you. Social media can help open up the possibilities. Our first workation was in Barcelona, where we had extremely generous friends who let us live with them and work out of their office. Since my college Spanish major had faded, they also helped with logistics, like renting a car and hiring a nanny, and answered our cultural questions.

Do you know someone who lives in a great location? Could you move in with them or could they give you recommendations on good neighborhoods, kids' activities, a work location, etc.?

Put out multiple requests on your social media channels to ask people if they have connections in the places you want to go. Your workation isn't someone else's priority, so don't feel bad about sending several reminders that you need help! (I typically get responses on the third try).

Do you have work connections somewhere else?

We chose London for a workation because my husband's employer had an office there, which made it easy for him to work and build new relationships within the company.

ACTION ITEM

Does your employer have an office abroad or in another state? Could you work out of it? Does the company you work for have a partner or subsidiary somewhere else? Could you work on-site for a customer?

Is language a factor?

I love the excitement of traveling in a country where English isn't the dominant language! But when dealing with as many logistics as we do for a workation (especially kid-related), I prefer an English-speaking country because I don't have any doubts about what's being communicated.

ACTION ITEM

Figure out whether the language matters to you. Are there any other languages that you or your partner speak? Do you have a friend in country who could help you out?

What's the time difference?

When we worked from New Zealand for six weeks, the time difference (19 hours ahead of our home time zone) was really tough. My husband got up regularly for conference calls at 3:30 a.m. and we worked on Saturdays (then took Sundays and Mondays off). For our next workation, we deliberately avoided a big time-change difference and life was much easier.

ACTION ITEM

Know what's realistic for you and think about how much flexibility you have to change your standing meetings/calls if needed. For me, I didn't want my clients to have to adjust or change anything just because I was traveling – but you may have different options or be able to set different expectations.

When's the best time to go?

When to leave and how long to be gone depend on your family's schedule. Maybe summer time is best when the kids are out of school. Maybe you're like me and live in a cold climate and want to get away in the winter and early spring.

Timing factors to consider:

- School schedules
- Work schedules (What are your slow times and busy times in a year?)
- Weather conditions where you live now (What would you need to do to prepare your home? If you leave in January, would you need to prevent your house pipes from freezing? Do you need someone to plow your driveway or check your furnace?)
- Weather conditions where you want to go (Is it the rainy season? Unbearably hot?)
- Tourist high or low seasons of your destination (and the impact on costs)

The world's a big place, but once you start prioritizing you can quickly narrow your choices. You can also find online resources to help you decide, such as <u>Nomad List</u>, which ranks cities by safety, places to work from, internet connections, etc. Take your time to make the right decision for your family.

ACTION ITEM
Using Worksheet A, narrow down your list of places to go.

My Story

My husband and I choose our workation destinations based on the variety of factors that have changed overtime. We took our very first workation in Barcelona because we had friends there who could provide us with lodging and fluent language assistance for logistics like child care and in-country travel.

For our next workations, we chose English-speaking countries because the shared language made us feel secure when organizing the logistics (especially related to our kids). Though there will always be funny moments, like the time that I stared blankly at our Kiwi nanny when she asked me if the boys had brought "togs." (those are swimsuits, by the way).

We chose New Zealand because it had been a place that we'd always wanted to visit. Because our oldest child was starting kindergarten the next year, we didn't know if we would be able to keep workationing. So the New Zealand trip had a live-life-to-the-fullest-because-we-don't-know-if-we'll-do-this-again intention to it.

But we DID do it again. Two years after New Zealand, we workationed in London. My husband's employer had an office there (see "My Husband's Story" in the previous chapter) and the time difference was much easier to manage than the 19-hour difference we experienced in New Zealand.

The season in which we workation is based on our Minnesota climate. I love Minnesota winters to an extent, but by February or March I'm ready to leave. We've taken our workations in the late winter or early spring so we can come back to a beautiful Minnesota summer. Other workationers I know love going abroad in the fall, when the tourist season is quieter in many parts of the world and travel is often cheaper.

The super glamorous part of a workation: late-night laundry!

A note on health insurance

Getting seriously sick or injured while in another country is a scary thought. For some families, this means workationing within the U.S. so you have the security of a health care system you know and that your insurance will cover. If you go abroad, research the health care system in your destination country.

- Call your health insurance provider and ask if they have resources or add-on plans for travelers abroad. We had Blue Cross Blue Shield insurance and they offer an app called <u>Global Core</u>, which helps you find doctors and hospitals outside of the U.S. that they cover.

- Once you have your housing confirmed, find the nearest clinic and hospital.
- In addition to prescription medications, you may want to buy over-the-counter medications once you arrive and have them on hand in-case someone gets sick in the middle of the night or reacts negatively to the new food, new environment, etc.
- If your destination has free public health care, you may be in good shape (but still research this ahead of time). When our 3-year-old seemed to be getting an ear infection just before our 32-hour trip home from New Zealand, I took him to a clinic. The total cost of the doctor visit and the prescription was $80 USD.

CHAPTER 5

The Money

"How do you afford it?"

Figuring out how to pay for a family workation is one of the biggest stressors for me. We save up for at least a year ahead of time. We sign up for travel credit cards that get us miles and points that we can cash in for airline tickets. We rarely eat out and we get brutal with our "needs vs wants" list. One year we could have replaced a window with a broken seal that fogged up so badly we couldn't see out of it...but we decided to travel instead.

The good part about this financial stress is that it's driven me to create a process around figuring out workation costs in different locations, which helps me pick our final workation destination.

Refer to Worksheet B: Comparing Workation Expenses at the end of this book to work through these items on your own and for pro tips.

<u>What are the approximate costs of your biggest expenses in your potential destinations?</u>
There's a huge range of what you'll spend on a workation, but these will likely be your biggest costs (not that dissimilar from your current lifestyle, probably).
- The flight
- Housing
- Child care or schooling (if needed)

- Work space (if needed)
- In-country transportation

Start with these four categories when comparing living expenses in the places you're considering.

ACTION ITEM

Use Worksheet B to research and compare the approximate costs for each location. Don't worry about finding the exact costs at this point – just get some ranges so you can compare the big numbers and narrow down your destination list further. If costs are very close between some destinations and you can't decide, then it will make sense to research the exact costs. Also, don't forget the exchange rate, which can play a major role in your daily costs.

Ask friends and acquaintances and social media networks for recommendations. Have friends traveled or lived in your potential workation spots already? Do they recommend any coworking spaces or neighborhoods? For our London workation, a friend's friend gave us a great recommendation for an affordable nanny agency.

Put out *several* requests for this information; asking once is usually not enough because people forget to answer, get busy, etc. I ask three times.

To determine the potential cost your workation, consider these key costs:

1. Flights
Start looking early so you can spot any trends in ticket prices.
- Look at your airline of choice and factor in any points you've accumulated (via credit cards, for instance) to help bring down the out-of-pocket cash cost.
- Use Google Flights or another tool to research destinations during the time of year you want to travel. Set up travel alerts for when prices drop or when good deals become available.

2. Housing
Tools like Airbnb or VRBO make it easy for you to get an idea of the costs of your lodging options.
- Consider whether you want to live in the city or a rural area. A rural area may have lots of charm, but you may also need a car, or have fewer options for a work space and child care.

- Do you have friends in another country that you could house-swap with?
- Search for local housing sites in the countries you're considering too. I found our stunning Wellington apartment by searching "furnished apartments Wellington" on Google and got in touch with an apartment management agency.

3. Work Space

Coworking is growing internationally and can serve as an affordable way to get a work space - and even make connections - in another place. I'll share more on this in the next chapter.

- Google "coworking" or "shared office space" in the city you're considering, or use a map like this to look into your options and the costs.
- Working from your temporary new home is another option if your kids are old enough to be self-sufficient, or you can find a daycare option for them that allows you to work from home while they're out of the house.

4. Child Care

This can be a big expense. I go into more detail about cost considerations in Chapter 7.

- Do a search for nanny or child care agencies if you have young kids.
- For now, limit your search to the top 2-3 that have the best reviews and appear to be the most credible to determine the potential cost. I've used KiwiOz Nannies (they serve New Zealand and Australia, or go here for their services in the UK) and Brilliant Nannies (in the UK) and have had great experiences with both.

5. Schooling

Depending on the age and maturity if your children, decide whether they can handle most of the school work on their own with some help from you, or whether they will need a more structured arrangement.

- If your kids need to keep up on school work, are they old enough to manage it on their own? Do you need to hire a nanny or tutor to help? Many nanny agencies also offer tutors.
- If your current school is affiliated with a larger network of schools, such as a religion or a teaching method like Montessori or Waldorf, are there schools in your destination city they could attend temporarily? If you want them enrolled in a school, you'll have to contact the potential schools and see what's realistic based on how long you're staying and any tuition.

6. In-Country Transportation

Most of us rely on our cars to get around during our day, and a workation is a great opportunity to experience the ease of public transportation systems in a foreign country. It always takes a few days to figure out the buses and trains, but I've found that most people working in the ticket booth are more than happy to explain to you how to buy a pass, help you figure out transfers, etc.

- Can you mostly take public transportation or will you have to rent a car? How much are rental rates? What type of car seat is required and what is the cost?
- Can you walk to work every day or will you spend an hour on the train? How much will you spend on commuting every day?

> **My Story**
> When we had to rent a car during part of our New Zealand trip, the costs were staggering. Minimizing transportation costs was a big factor when I planned our next workation.

7. Currency Exchange Rate

Factor in the exchange rates to figure out where your dollar will stretch the farthest. Just because one country's costs may be a bit higher than another, the exchange rate could narrow the difference. (here's a <u>currency converter</u>)

ACTION ITEM

Complete Worksheets A and B and make some decisions!

Your destination

The time of year to travel

How long to be gone

CHAPTER 6

Choosing Where to Live and Work

"How do you find a place to live?
That sounds scary!"

Before working through this chapter, go back to the intention you wrote down in Chapter 4. What do you want to get out of your workation? What sort of new or better family routines do you want it to support?

I already mentioned that our workation intention is to flip our lifestyle. Our home is in a quiet, rural, homogenous community. When we travel, we want a big city that is bustling and diverse. I want to simplify my life and live within walking distance of grocery stores, parks, restaurants and shops. I want to be able to walk to work or take public transportation. And I want to be able to talk with and make new connections with the people around me.

Therefore, it's essential that I live close to where I will be working. I structure my workation around the location of my work space.

For this part of your plan, use Worksheet C: Choosing Where to Live and Work to work through the Action Items listed here.

First, pick the space that you're going to work out of. I don't recommend coffee shops or just winging it unless you're 100% confident about your internet connection and cultural norms. For example, I've found plenty of coffee shops with unreliable internet. When we were in Spain, we were told it wasn't appropriate or normal to hang out at a coffee shop all day to work.

Simply working from your new home could be a possibility depending on the internet connection and whether having your kids and nanny around will disrupt your work. In my situation, my kids were at the house for several hours each day, so that would've been a big distraction. I also wanted the experience of meeting new people. That's why I decided to join a coworking space. Coworking is a growing workplace model across the world (go here to find spaces around the globe). You can find posh places or simple spreads where you can work in a community of locals who enhance your workation experience.

Coworking spaces usually have different membership levels, such as five days a week or three days a week. I get a four-day membership (I work from my workation home on Fridays), and I've been able to get custom memberships (and rates) simply by contacting the coworking company, explaining my temporary work situation, and asking what they can offer. Almost every single one I've contacted has been accommodating. So, if you're not sure or you don't see exactly what you want, just ask.

My London coworking space.

My Story: Choosing a Work Space

A coworking space is simply a shared workplace. It's a large office or building that offers flexible "memberships" to small companies or individuals. These memberships usually include a desk or some sort of work space (dedicated or undedicated), internet, and sometimes amenities like beverages and access to a printer.

I don't spend a lot of time choosing a coworking location, as I can usually get a really quick idea of availability and costs with a few simple web searches and emails. I've worked in posh coworking spaces and pretty sparse ones, and I think of them more as a means for getting my work done and meeting new people, rather than how trendy the desks are or how many foosball tables they have.

After I have the coworking space picked, I use Google Maps and figure out a 30-minute commute radius around the coworking spot. In other words, I don't want to commute more than 30 minutes on my workation, whether that's on foot or on a bus or by train. Even if an apartment costs more because of its location, it's worth it if the location significantly cuts down on my commute time and cost. Why exchange a brutal American commute for a brutal foreign one?

For our London workation, it was a bit trickier because my husband and I were working in two different locations and that was something we hadn't done before. So I had to find a neighborhood that was no more than a 30-minute commute from his office or from mine. Because London is such a big city with so many coworking spaces, I found a great neighborhood that was a 30-minute bus ride for him and that had two coworking options for me, each about a 15-minute walk from our flat.

My husband's commute.

I use a combination of Airbnb and Google maps to figure out neighborhood options.

<u>What to do with your house while you're away</u>
Some workationers put their home up for rent while they're away (note that there are tax implications if you do this, so check with an accountant or tax advisor); others invite friends to live in their home (either paid or just to house sit). There are multiple ways you could rent out your home and earn some extra income while you're gone – and maybe even pay for your housing abroad! I'd also recommend some sort of security system while you're away for extra peace of mind.

ACTION ITEM
Using Worksheet C, decide on your neighborhood and housing, and your work location!

CHAPTER 7

Child Care

"I could never leave my kids with a stranger
in a foreign city!"

If your children are young enough to need some sort of child care, finding it can be the most nerve-wracking part of planning a workation. Even though each nanny we've ever interviewed has seemed great, I always have the same feeling right before we meet her in person: "Are we crazy for leaving our kids with a total stranger in a foreign city?!" In fact, I think child care is the big reason a lot of families who could workation won't – they're too afraid to make that leap.

You know your child best, so what I can offer here are a lot of ideas and real-life stories of how other families have done it.

> **My Story**
> *Finding someone to care for my kids in a foreign country isn't that different than finding child care in the United States. I gauge how responsive and well-presented the agency is, I ask for references for the nanny, I look into how well the nannies are screened and what credentials are required, and my husband and I interview them via Skype at least once before making a decision.*

Child Care: Nanny or Daycare?

While I've always hired a nanny to care for our children, a daycare is another option. I've tried this in every city we've workationed in and have always been turned down because they don't want to accept kids for just a few weeks. But I'd still recommend reaching out to a daycare if you find one online that appeals to you.

If you go the nanny route, the most important thing you can do is find a reputable child care agency with stellar references. They should clearly list the credentials required of their nannies and screen them as if they were working for the Secret Service. (I'm going to refer to all nannies as "her/she" because the vast majority of nannies we've interacted with and reviewed are female).

Use Worksheet D: Finding a Nanny, to work through finding an agency and nanny.

Although a nanny is more expensive than a daycare, I like using nannies because they have always been very flexible, convenient (they come right to the apartment rather than me having to drop off the kids somewhere) and they've essentially been a private tour guide for our kids, showing them neighborhoods and teaching them things about the local city that neither my husband nor I ever got to experience! Nothing beats coming home from work to hear my son explain that the name "Big Ben" actually refers to the bell inside that tower, not the clock or tower itself.

Finding a nanny agency is something you should start early on in the planning process. Identify what agency you'll use and then be prepared to wait until 3-4 months before your departure to actually start interviewing and make your selection. This is because temporary nannies (those you hire for a few weeks or months) can change frequently, and the agency usually won't know who's available from their roster until closer to your departure date.

As you find reputable agencies, start asking them questions related to:
- How they screen candidates
- All of their costs and fees (will they charge you a fee just to find the nanny? Is there an enrollment fee?)

- How taxes are handled (THIS IS IMPORTANT. I handled taxes myself for one of our workations and it was so confusing and so much work, I will never do it myself again. So ask: Does the nanny agency handle all taxes related to employing a nanny, or are you responsible for them?) (Read more on my experience with nanny taxes)
- What happens if the nanny doesn't work out and you need to make a change? (On our first workation, our nanny suddenly told us she couldn't work anymore, but the agency was terrific about finding us an even better nanny right away.)

How the process usually works

Once I find an agency I want to work with, I tell the agency where I'm staying in the city, how long I'll be there and our expectations of the nanny. There's usually a form to fill out about your children's ages, interests, temperaments, medical conditions, etc. From there, the agency shares your information with potential nannies, and those interested submit their resumes or CVs. The agency will forward you the applications and you can review them and decide which nannies you want to interview.

Here are some steps I take when hiring a nanny:

1. Evaluate Experience

How long has this person been in the child care field? Is this their career, or just something they're doing to get by for a few months? Does the person have experience caring for a diversity of ages, genders and number of children at one time? Maybe they've cared for an infant, but do they have experience handling two school-aged boys?

2. Consult References

Make sure the agency gives you references or testimonials for the potential nanny. Contact the references directly with more questions like:
- How was your experience with this person?
- Was she responsive?
- Was she prompt?
- How did she mesh with the children?
- Tell me about your child's typical day with her.
- What were your expectations for her?
- Did she meet your expectations?

3. Interview for Fit

We interview nannies on Skype so we can see them face to face. Here are some of the questions we ask...

- Tell us about yourself.
- Why did you decide to become a nanny?
- What's your approach to discipline? What do you do?
- What's been a challenging family situation and how did you deal with it?
- How familiar are you with the neighborhood/area where we'll be living?
- We also explain how we want our children's day to be structured (at least half day of outdoor play or touring the city, and a few hours spent on school work). But we also leave the nanny leeway to see what works best for the kids. Our wonderful nanny in London found that giving the boys physical activity in the morning helped them focus better on school work in the afternoon.

Set clear expectations about spending. If you give her $25 for the day, be explicit about whether you want her to spend all of it. The best nanny we've had was extremely thrifty (like packing lunches for the kids instead of buying food) and asking us ahead of time about her ideas for trips and tours, so we could approve the cost. She also documented how much cash I gave her, how much she spent each day and why, and how much cash remained.

Expect to pay your nanny's way into museums, tours etc. I also buy the nanny a bus or train pass to use when she's traveling with the kids. In my experience, that isn't expected but it's a nice gesture.

Here's what our boys' typical day looked like when they were five and seven years old (preschool and first grade):

- Spend the first half of the day at a park, museum, or some other activity like a trampoline park, local educational festival, etc.
- In the afternoon and with the nanny's guidance, spend an hour or two working on reading, math lessons, workbooks and brain teasers that I brought for them. They also played chess or checkers, and wrote or drew pictures about their day (which make for great keepsakes!). One of my son's sweetest journal entries was about the day the nanny took them to 10 Downing Street where the U.K. Prime Minister lives (you can't get very close to the residence because of security), and my son wrote in his journal "Today we went to see the Prime Minister!"

For each of our workations, the boys have sent a postcard to their teacher and classmates explaining what they are learning. When we return to the States, the boys turn in their journals and talk about what they learned. Notably, the kids reintegrate back into their classrooms quite well. They are a little nervous on the first day back ("What if I forgot where my locker is?!" said my oldest son), but by Day 2 they are SO excited to be back with their friends that it's like they never left.

ACTION ITEM
If using a nanny, use Worksheet D to search for and decide on the right nanny for your family. Or decide on the schooling option that will work best.

CHAPTER 8

This is Happening!

You now have the questions, ideas, and resources for jump-starting your workation plans! There are a LOT of logistics to plan for and things to keep track of, so in the Appendix of this book there are several worksheets and resources to help you stay organized:

- A worksheet that compiles all of the Action Items listed throughout the book
- A suggested timeline of what to do and when, including options for writing in your own timeline
- A packing list
- An expense comparison chart
- A list of suggested nanny interview questions
- An essentials check list of important but not-so-obvious information to have and know before you leave

You are going to make this happen! Stay diligent!

And don't forget: A workation doesn't have to mean six months overseas. For your family, maybe it means spending two weeks at a cabin on a lake and working from there. I hope to head to Hawaii for a few weeks next year and work out of our condo for part of the time. Working for a few hours each day is a small sacrifice that allows our family to enjoy a beautiful new location for a longer period of time!

The going will get hard: There will be a lot of planning and lots of tough decisions. Go back to your intention that you wrote out at the beginning of this book and reflect on what this trip means to your family and what you hope to learn from it! Your routines, your assumptions, and even your parenting may be changed forever. And that's a wonderful thing!

I'd love to hear your questions, lessons learned and successes! Be sure to read more about my experiences, recommendations and find more resources at <u>Workation Woman</u> *(that's www.workationwoman.com). You can also drop me a note on my* <u>Facebook page</u> *or write me at* <u>maria@workationwoman.com</u>*!*

This was the best family photo we could manage that day. (Edinburgh, Scotland)

APPENDIX OF RESOURCES

For more user-friendly versions of these worksheets, download and print PDF versions of them all at www.workationwoman.com

WORKSHEET A

Choose Where and When (See Chapter 4)

Narrow down the options of where to go and the time of year to be gone.

Step 1: Where to go?

Write down your dream workation destinations – up to ten of them.

1.
2.
3.
4.
5.
6.
7.
8.
9.
10.

Now start thinking through and journaling about these factors to help you figure out which locations are the best fit and most realistic.

Do you know someone who lives in any of these locations? If so, which ones?

_____

_____

_____

_____

_____

Could you (or would you want to) live with the people you know in these locations?

_____

_____

_____

_____

_____

_____

Does your employer have an office, partner/subsidiary or a client location there that you could work out of?

_____

_____

_____

_____

_____

_____

Is the country's language(s) a factor? (considering other languages you or your partner may speak)

_____

_____

_____

_____

_____

_____

What's the time difference? Do you have much flexibility (or desire) to change meeting times or conference calls for work, or are you willing to get up at 3:00am or work on weekends to make up for the time change?

_____

_____

_____

_____

_____

_____

Narrow your list down to your top 3-5 locations

1.

2.

3.

4.

5.

Step 2: When to go?

Which months do you want to travel?

_____

_____

_____

_____

_____

_____

_____

_____

_____

_____

Which of these months, if any, are off limits because of family or work commitments, weather, school schedules or extra-curriculars? Cross them off the list above.

Consider special house preparations you would need to do while you're gone during your potential months. (If you live in a cold climate and are gone in January, do you need someone to check your furnace or pipes?)

_____

_____

_____

_____

_____

For the locations you're considering, what's happening during the months you want to travel? Is it a tourist high season or low season? Rainy season or particularly hot or cold? Do a quick online search to find out if there are any large festivals or holiday weeks that will make your time there more expensive or logistically challenging.

_____

_____

_____

_____

_____

List the best months that remain:

_____

_____

_____

_____

_____

Pro Tip

Put out multiple requests on social media and ask friends if they have connections in these locations to help with neighborhoods, activity ideas, etc.

WORKSHEET B

Compare Workation Expenses
(See Chapter 5)

Start comparing the major expenses of a workation
and decide on a location that makes sense for your family.

Remember: Don't worry about finding the exact costs at this point – just get some ranges so you can compare the big numbers and narrow down your destination list further. If costs are very close between some destinations and you can't decide, then it will make sense to research the exact costs.

Refer to Chapter 5 for links and ideas for researching your major workation expenses:

- Flights
- Housing
- Work space or office space (if needed)
- Child care or schooling (if needed)
- In-country transportation

Location #1

	Cost	Notes
Flight		
Housing		
Work space for X weeks		
Schooling		
Nanny (incl agency fee & taxes)		
Transportation (bus fares, car rental, etc.)		
Other expenses (specific to your family)		
Other Expenses (specific to your family)		
Currency exchange rate		
TOTALS		
Other factors		
Time difference		
Season/time of year		
Health care		

	Cost	Notes
Flight		
Housing		
Work space for X weeks		
Schooling		
Nanny (incl agency fee & taxes)		
Transportation (bus fares, car rental, etc.)		
Other expenses (specific to your family)		
Other Expenses (specific to your family)		
Currency exchange rate		
TOTALS		
Other factors		
Time difference		
Season/time of year		
Health care		

	Cost	Notes
Flight		
Housing		
Work space for X weeks		
Schooling		
Nanny (incl agency fee & taxes)		
Transportation (bus fares, car rental, etc.)		
Other expenses (specific to your family)		
Other Expenses (specific to your family)		
Currency exchange rate		
TOTALS		
Other factors		
Time difference		
Season/time of year		
Health care		

Pro Tips

You may feel like you should buy things like bus passes or train passes months in advance, but that's not always cost-effective, especially if you don't really know what your daily routine will be. We wait until we arrive in the country and get a feel for a typical day before committing to a type of transit pass.

A common practice is to exchange money in the U.S. and then travel. However, we've gotten much better exchange rates and saved a ton of money by finding a bank or even an ATM in our destination country to exchange dollars. We do exchange a minimal amount of money head of time, like $20 for some sort of emergency or a tip for a driver. We also rely on credit cards with no foreign transaction fees. Another traveler I know uses a Charles Schwab investment account with ATM chip card, which allows you to transfer a certain amount of your bank account to be accessed overseas (so your whole bank account isn't at risk).

NOW, based on Worksheets A and B, plus any help or connections you've been able to get through friends and family, it's time to make decisions!

Destination: _____

Time of year to travel: _____

How long to be gone: _____

WORKSHEET C

Choose Where to Live and Work
(See Chapter 6)

If you don't have a neighborhood or work space in mind already,
use this worksheet to narrow your options.

See Chapter 6 and do a search for work spaces or coworking spaces. Based on location, price and amenities, list them here.

Work Space	Location	Cost	Pros	Cons	Notes

More notes/considerations:

_____
_____
_____
_____
_____

Based on the table above, choose your top one or two work spaces.

Choice #1: _____

Choice #2: _____

Next, use Google Maps or another tool and figure out your max commute radius around the work space. Mine is always 30 minutes; in other words, I don't want to commute more than 30 minutes on my workation, whether that's on foot or on a bus or by train.

Now, choose 1-3 neighborhoods and begin your actual housing search (see Chapter 5). Write out your options and notes here.

Neighborhood	Cost	Pros	Cons	Notes

More notes/considerations:

_____

_____

_____

_____

_____

_____

Pro Tip

To build a sense of community in your new neighborhood, look for a café, house of worship, or gym nearby where you become a "regular." In Wellington, we did the same yoga class four days a week and were soon recognizing our fellow classmates in other places throughout the city!

NOW, decide on your in-country housing and work location!

Housing: _____

Work space: _____

WORKSHEET D

Find a Nanny (See Chapter 7)

Work through the process of finding
an agency and hiring a nanny.

The most important thing you can do is find a reputable child care agency with stellar references. Using internet searches and personal references, find 2-3 reputable nanny agencies (side note: many nannies register with multiple agencies, so you don't need to go overboard and search for a million agencies).

List them here.

_____

_____

_____

Finding a nanny agency is something you should start early on in the planning process. Identify what agency you'll use but be prepared to wait until 3-4 months before your departure to actually start interviewing and make your selection. This is because temporary nannies (those you hire for a few weeks or months) can change frequently, and the agency won't know who's available from their roster until closer to your departure date.

Next, contact the agencies and start asking them questions such as:

1. How do you screen your candidates?
2. How are your costs and fees structured? (do they charge a fee just to find the nanny? Is there an enrollment fee?)

3. How taxes are handled (THIS IS IMPORTANT. Does the nanny agency handle all taxes related to employing a nanny, or are you responsible for them?) (Read my experience with nanny taxes)
4. What happens if the nanny doesn't work out and you need to make a change?

Agency Name	Approx. Cost	Pros	Cons	Notes

Sample Nanny Interview Questions
1. Tell us about yourself.
2. Why did you decide to become a nanny?
3. Why do you like being a nanny? What challenges you the most about your job?
4. What are the typical ages and genders of the children you've cared for?
5. What's your approach to discipline? What do you do?
6. What's been a challenging family situation and how did you deal with it?
7. How familiar are you with the neighborhood/area where we'll be living?
8. Discuss how you want your children's day to be structured, but allow the nanny to give her own ideas and recommendations too.

Sample Questions for Nanny References
1. How was your experience with this person?
2. Was she responsive?
3. Was she prompt?
4. How did she mesh with the children?
5. Tell me about your child's typical day with her.
6. What were your expectations for her?
7. Did she meet your expectations?

WORKSHEET E

The Workation Woman Timeline

(Remember: All of these worksheets can be downloaded at
www.workationwoman.com)

This is the approximate timeline I used when planning our first workation, and it's a great start if you're just beginning to consider workation possibilities. I've included suggested timing, but fill in what's realistic for you and celebrate each time you can check off the "Completed" column!

Suggested Timing: 18 Months Out	Your Timing:
☐ **COMPLETED**	**Action:** Start thinking about where and when you want to workation. **Resources:** Chapter 4 **Notes:**

Suggested Timing: 18 Months Out	Your Timing:
☐ **COMPLETED**	**Action:** Sign up for a mileage-accruing credit card to help with flight costs. **Resources:** Start accruing airline miles to help with flight costs. I use the Delta SkyMiles Amex card and other workationers I know like the Capital One Venture card (which can be used for any airline). And you don't always need to accrue the total amount for a ticket; some airlines let you use miles to pay for

	part of the ticket and pay less out of pocket. Another resource I use a lot is the <u>Points Guy.</u>
	Notes:

Suggested Timing: 12 Months Out	**Your Timing:**
☐ **COMPLETED**	**Action:** Decide where and when you want to go. **Resources:** Chapters 4-6 **Notes:**

Suggested Timing: 12 Months Out	**Your Timing:**
☐ **COMPLETED**	**Action:** Make sure you have all passports, visas and travel documents required (and that they're current!) **Resources:** Consider signing up for <u>Global Entry</u> or <u>Mobile Passport Control</u>. **Notes:**

Suggested Timing: 12 Months Out	**Your Timing:**
☐ **COMPLETED**	**Action:** If you have school-aged kids, talk to the school about your plans. **Resources:** Chapter 3 **Notes:**

Suggested Timing: 12-9 Months Out	**Your Timing:**

☐ **COMPLETED**	**Action:** Ask your employer about working remotely. **Resources:** Chapter 2 **Notes:**

Suggested Timing: 12-9 Months Out	**Your Timing:**

☐ **COMPLETED**	**Action:** Decide on a work space and neighborhood. **Resources:** Chapter 6 **Notes:**

Suggested Timing: 12-9 Months Out	**Your Timing:**

☐ **COMPLETED**	**Action:** Finalize your housing. **Resources:** Chapter 6 **Notes:**

Suggested Timing: 9-3 Months Out	**Your Timing:**

☐ **COMPLETED**	**Action:** Book a flight. **Resources:** Think about the number of stops and the time between stops. A 3-hour layover can be a good thing because it gives you a buffer in case your first flight is running late, and the kids can stretch their legs. **Notes:**

Suggested Timing: 5-3 Months Out	Your Timing:
☐ **COMPLETED**	**Action:** Confirm child care or schooling **Resources:** Chapter 3 and 7 **Notes:**

Suggested Timing: 3 Months Out	Your Timing:
☐ **COMPLETED**	**Action:** Make a list of ways you can save money while you're gone. **Resources:** Chapter 5; The Essentials Checklist (Appendix); <u>Six Ways to Cut Costs</u> **Notes:**

Suggested Timing: 2 Months Out	Your Timing:
☐ **COMPLETED**	**Action:** Research health care options in your new location. **Resources:** Chapter 4 **Notes:**

Suggested Timing: 2 Months Out	**Your Timing:**
□ **COMPLETED**	**Action:** Call your cell phone carrier and figure out international usage; should you get an international plan, pay as needed, or just rely on free Wi-Fi? **Resources:** **Notes:**

Suggested Timing: 2 Months Out	**Your Timing:**
□ **COMPLETED**	**Action:** If needed, apply for an international driving permit. **Resources:** Check out <u>AAA</u> **Notes:**
Suggested Timing: 2 Months Out	**Your Timing:**
□ **COMPLETED**	**Action:** Get a small gift for the nanny or anyone else. **Resources:** Not required, but a nice gesture. **Notes:**
Suggested Timing: 2 Months – 2 Weeks Out	**Your Timing:**
□ **COMPLETED**	**Action:** Book your work space. **Resources:** Chapter 6 (Check to see how early you should book a membership) **Notes:**

Suggested Timing: 5-3 Weeks Out	**Your Timing:**
☐ **COMPLETED**	**Action:** Contact nanny to confirm all schedules. **Resources:** **Notes:**
Suggested Timing: 4 Weeks Out	**Your Timing:**
☐ **COMPLETED**	**Action:** Start your packing list. **Resources:** Worksheet F **Notes:**

Suggested Timing: 4-3 Weeks Out	**Your Timing:**
☐ **COMPLETED**	**Action:** Dig out clothes/jackets that you will need to bring. Does everything fit? What needs to be washed? Do any of the kids need new sandals/shorts/jackets? Get those now. **Resources:** **Notes:**

Suggested Timing: 3 Weeks Out	**Your Timing:**
☐ **COMPLETED**	**Action:** Schedule all last-minute appointments: Haircuts, oil changes, dentists, etc. **Resources:** Worksheet G for the important but not-so-obvious tasks to complete before you leave.

	Notes:

Suggested Timing: 3 Weeks Out	Your Timing:
☐ **COMPLETED**	**Action:** Confirm everything with your host/housing; ask any last-minute questions. Book in-country car rentals and figure out how to get from airport to apartment (book something ahead of time if needed). **Resources:** **Notes:**

Suggested Timing: 2 Weeks Out	Your Timing:
☐ **COMPLETED**	**Action:** Confirm house-sitting details or who's checking on your house. **Resources:** **Notes:**

Suggested Timing: 2 Weeks Out	Your Timing:
☐ **COMPLETED**	**Action:** Put newspaper on hold; garbage/recycle on hold; figure out how to handle all bills and paychecks while you're gone; set up mail to be forwarded; ensure you have enough money to cover surprises. **Resources:** <u>Handling Bills, Paychecks and Mail</u>, Worksheet G **Notes:**

Suggested Timing: 2 Weeks Out	**Your Timing:**
☐ **COMPLETED**	**Action:** Double check your technology: Do you have the right converters and adapters (<u>we like this one</u>) for your computers, phones, iPads, e-readers? How many things can you charge at once? Do you need to buy anything extra? **Resources:** <u>Staying Connected while Abroad</u> <u>My Favorite Apps & Sites</u> **Notes:**

Suggested Timing: 1 Week Out	**Your Timing:**
☐ **COMPLETED**	**Action:** Give valuables to a family member so they're not sitting in your house while you're gone; call banks and credit cards to let them know you're going overseas; pick-up any extra prescriptions; bring a little bit of cash in the foreign currency and exchange more overseas. **Resources:** <u>Handling Bills, Paychecks and Mail</u> **Notes:**

Suggested Timing: 2-1 Week Out	**Your Timing:**
☐ **COMPLETED**	**Action:** Add a new time zone to your online calendar so you can see whether you need to reschedule meetings, etc. Get into the mindset of when you'll be working as compared to your

	coworkers/employees/clients. **Resources:** Last-Minute Jitters **Notes:**

Suggested Timing: During the Workation	**Your Timing:**
□ **COMPLETED**	**Action:** Ask a question or share your experience on my Facebook page! I'd love to hear from you! **Resources:** Schedule Examples Cooking (and Eating) as a Digital Nomad Family **Notes:**

Suggested Timing: 1 Week after Returning	**Your Timing:**
□ **COMPLETED**	**Action:** Chill. Don't schedule anything. Don't rush to get back into a routine. Reflect on your time away and your intention for the trip: Do you need a NEW routine? What did you do differently on your travels that you want to bring back home? But do laundry. You'll definitely need to do laundry. **Resources:** Lifestyle Changes after a Workation **Notes:**

	Suggested Timing: 3 Weeks after Returning Your Timing:
☐ **COMPLETED**	**Action:** Bills will start coming and may be overwhelming. Go back to your intention and remember why you did this! **Resources:** **Notes:**

	Suggested Timing: 2 Months after Returning Your Timing:
☐ **COMPLETED**	**Action:** Start dreaming and planning the next workation. **Resources:** **Notes:**

WORKSHEET F

The Workation Woman Packing List

We don't buy fancy travel gear or gadgets when we workation. The biggest thing to remember when packing is that people live where you are going! So unless you're going somewhere really remote, you'll be able to buy ibuprofen, diapers, clothes and toys once you get there. If you have friends living nearby, see if they have supplies you can borrow like a car seat or pack n' play.

Use this list to get your own packing started, and I've included lines for you to add your own items!

The Luggage List
- [ ] 1 big suitcase for your clothes/shoes/toiletries
- [ ] 1 big suitcase for your spouse's clothes/shoes/toiletries
- [ ] 1 big suitcase for every two kids' clothes/shoes/toiletries (age dependent)
- [ ] 1 extra suitcase for kids' toys, work files and supplies, kids supplies (like diapers) etc. If you have the space, pack more toys than you think they'll need. They'll like the comforts of home and will be less likely to ask for screens for entertainment.
- [ ] 1 carry-on bag per person (including kids) that has snacks and distractions for the plane like small toys, a deck of cards, electronics, etc.
- [ ] Carry-on laptop for you (if needed)
- [ ] Carry-on laptop for your spouse (if needed)
- [ ] _____
- [ ] _____
- [ ] _____
- [ ] _____

Your Suitcase/Spouse's Suitcase

- ☐ 3-4 shirts, weather-appropriate
- ☐ 2-3 pants/shorts
- ☐ 1 nice outfit for a fancier restaurant or event
- ☐ 1 warm jacket
- ☐ 1 rain jacket
- ☐ Hats and gloves or mittens
- ☐ Sun hat
- ☐ 2-3 pairs of shoes (1 for everyday walking; 1 pair of tennis shoes or hiking shoes; 1 nice pair of shoes to go with the nice outfit)
- ☐ Work-out clothes if you're planning to run, join a gym, join a yoga studio, etc.
- ☐ Five pairs of underwear
- ☐ Five pairs of socks
- ☐ Bras
- ☐ 1 week's worth of toiletries: Travel-sized shampoo/conditioner, toothpaste, a few Band-Aids, a small amount of sunscreen, etc. Buy the full-sized supplies once you've arrived.
- ☐ Favorite recipes (I explain why here)
- ☐ A NICE camera. Don't only rely on your phone: This might be the trip of a lifetime, so invest in or borrow a good camera that will take pictures you can enlarge when you return home.
- ☐ Cords and power adapters (we like this universal adapter plug)
- ☐ Optional: A small gift for the nanny. I always like to give her something small and meaningful at the end of her time with us, such as a piece of jewelry made by a Minnesota artist.
- ☐ _____
- ☐ _____
- ☐ _____
- ☐ _____
- ☐ _____
- ☐ _____
- ☐ _____

Your Kids' Suitcase

- ☐ 4-5 shirts, weather-appropriate
- ☐ 3-4 pants/shorts
- ☐ 1 nicer shirt for a fancier restaurant or event
- ☐ 1 warm jacket
- ☐ 1 rain jacket

- ☐ Hats and gloves or mittens
- ☐ Sun hat
- ☐ 1 pair of tennis shoes
- ☐ 7 pairs of socks
- ☐ 7 pairs of underwear
- ☐ 1 week's worth of toiletries
- ☐ _____
- ☐ _____
- ☐ _____
- ☐ _____
- ☐ _____
- ☐ _____
- ☐ _____

Extra Suitcase (pack lightly to use this for souvenirs on the way home)

- ☐ Kids toys
- ☐ Work files/supplies (use electronic versions as much as you can)
- ☐ Other supplies that take up a lot of space, like a few days' worth of diapers if needed
- ☐ School work
- ☐ _____
- ☐ _____
- ☐ _____
- ☐ _____
- ☐ _____
- ☐ _____
- ☐ _____

Carry-on Bags

- ☐ Snacks
- ☐ One outfit change for each person
- ☐ Toothbrush
- ☐ Prescriptions
- ☐ Any valuables in case suitcases are lost
- ☐ All travel documents and hard copies of all of your confirmations for housing, coworking, important phone numbers, directions for getting from the airport to your housing, etc. Don't assume your phone will work or connect once you land!
- ☐ Small toys, deck of cards, workbooks, other distractions for the plane
- ☐ Phones, iPads, e-readers and all chargers

☐   Toiletries (especially wipes for cleaning hands and spills)

☐   _____

☐   _____

☐   _____

Pro Tips

I pack at least 1-2 shirts that I don't really like and I pack my oldest, grossest pair of tennis shoes. When it's time to leave, I either throw the clothes/shoes away or donate them, depending on the condition. That frees up even more suitcase space for souvenirs on the way home.

Our boys each take one backpack on the flight, and they can pack any toys they want. But they MUST carry their own bag the entire time – my husband and I have enough to lug around! So after they've packed their backpacks, we make the boys walk all around our house to test their bags' weight. Usually, they end up removing at least a few items!

After you arrive, buy a soccer ball or another sort of ball that the kids can kick around your backyard or the local park. It takes up a lot of room if you decide to bring it back home, but it's totally worth it while you're in the new city.

WORKSHEET G

The Essential-but-not-Obvious To-Do List

There are a million details to remember before you head out on a workation. Here's the checklist I use to make sure I have some of those less obvious (but important) ones covered. There are also many blank lines for you to add your own!

Before You Go

- ☐ Called banks and credit card companies to tell them where you're traveling (so they don't assume fraudulent activity when you try to buy a bag of chips in Buenos Aires)
- ☐ Redirected mail (see here for more details)
- ☐ Researched health insurance coverage in workation destination
- ☐ Removed all-but-minimum car insurance (saves $$)
- ☐ Put house internet and cable on hold (saves $$)
- ☐ Called your mobile phone carrier and figured out international phone usage. Should you get an international plan, pay as needed, or just rely on free Wi-Fi?
- ☐ Security system/plans in place
- ☐ Have scheduled someone to regularly check on the house and check mailbox in case something slips through post office
- ☐ Put garbage/recycle pick-up on hold
- ☐ Ordered extra prescriptions to take with
- ☐ If needed, got an International Driving Permit (see AAA)
- ☐ Gave valuables to family member so they're not in your house while you're gone

- ☐ Exchanged a small amount of cash so you have $25-$100 in foreign currency before you leave
- ☐ Put local newspaper delivery on hold (nothing says "I'm not home, please rob me" like a pile of newspapers at your front door)
- ☐ _____
- ☐ _____
- ☐ _____
- ☐ _____
- ☐ _____
- ☐ _____
- ☐ _____
- ☐ _____

To Take with You

- ☐ Hard copies of all of your travel documents, including confirmations for your housing, work space, and directions for getting from the airport to your home. Don't assume your phone will work or connect once you land!
- ☐ Contact name and number for your housing
- ☐ Contact name and number for nanny agency or school
- ☐ Contact name and number for nanny
- ☐ Name, number and address of nearest hospital
- ☐ Name, number and address of nearest clinic
- ☐ Name, number of any local friends or friends of friends, in case of emergency
- ☐ _____
- ☐ _____
- ☐ _____
- ☐ _____
- ☐ _____
- ☐ _____
- ☐ _____
- ☐ _____
- ☐ _____

Made in the USA
Middletown, DE
16 December 2019